Celebrating Our Nation

C is for Canada

Written by Mike Ulmer and Illustrated by Sylvie Daigneault

A is for Aurora Borealis

Look up into the nighttime sky
    and see the colours dance on by.
The show takes place on cloudless nights;
    Aurora Borealis means Northern Lights.

B is for Beaver

Our national symbol has little toes,
little eyes and a little nose.
But his heart is big; he's always eager—
Canada is like that busy beaver.

C is for Canada

Canada is busy cities, peaceful creeks,
cool, wet forests and bustling streets.
Where winter's alive with the sharp sound of skates
and the call of the loon breaks the quiet of the lake.

D is for Dinosaur

If you like taking pictures and want some new friends,
and you favour nice tall ones who'll fill up the lens,
head off to Alberta—there're big ones to meet.
I hope you like dinosaurs with big pointy teeth.

E is for Edgewalk

Those floors must be awfully high,
floating far up in the sky.
The CN Tower's walkabout
puts the hang in hanging out.

F is for Football

I love football in lots of ways:
    I love the runs and punts and plays.
  It's best when a fumble hits the ground
    and we dive in the mud and roll around.

G is for Gravy

It's warm and delicious and easy to make
and tops off poutine like icing on cake.
It covers the outside like bark does on wood;
I'd slurp up that gravy with a straw if I could.

H is for Husky

A husky's never happier
than when charging through the snow.
The sun is up and the dogs want out;
their barking says, "Let's go!"

I is for Island Hymn

Lucy wrote a simple song about her Island home
   and Islanders now know the song, and often sing along.
So when you go to PEI, please also understand
   the pen that wrote the Island Hymn also gave us Anne.

J is for Blue Jays

Blue Jays are a sneaky bird;
they'll steal second base and then steal third.
And swipe home runs off the other team's bats
by scaling the fence and bringing them back.

Underneath the summer sun
    K-Days brings a world of fun.
So grab your sunscreen and your shades
    and soak up all those summer rays.

K is for Klondike Days

L is for Loonies and Toonies

The sound of it gives me a smile
  when I add a coin every once in a while.
A loonie makes a lovely "clank"
  when dropped inside my piggy bank.

Our country's like a maple tree—
we know the strongest limbs
are those with roots that reach around
the world and back again.

M is for Maple Leaf

N is for National Hockey League

To play in the NHL would be a thrill
but first I have to learn one skill.
I can skate very fast, I'm off like a shot—
I just need to learn the best way to stop.

O is for Osprey

They're brown and white with a yellow eye
  and favour homes that are oceanside.
So they can go out when they wish
  and bring their babies fresh-caught fish.

P is for Peary Caribou

They look quite slow
    as they're chewing on grass,
but you ought to know
        these caribou are fast!

Q is for Quebec City

A stone fort called the Citadelle,
a grand and wonderful hotel,
walls to climb, an aquarium to see–
Quebec is the perfect city for me!

R is for Rock Rabbits

When a rock rabbit lets out a squeak,
  it means it's playing hide-and-seek.
And when it gives another cry,
  it means it's safe to go outside.

S is for Science Centre

The Science Centre's
the place to go.
There sure isn't much
that they don't know!

T is for Trout

Dolly Varden—that's a funny name,
even for a fish.
You catch them in the western streams,
release them if you wish.

U is for Underwear

We treasure pretty Truro,
I think we always will.
   That's where they make the long johns
that protect us from the chill.

V is for Victoria

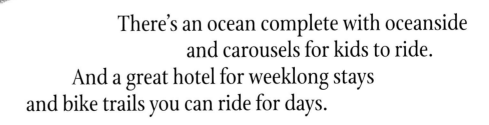

There's an ocean complete with oceanside
and carousels for kids to ride.
And a great hotel for weeklong stays
and bike trails you can ride for days.

W is for Whale Watching

Except for lunches filled with krill,
to be a whale would be a thrill.
The best part is there is no rule
that whales must spend their days in schools.

X is for Camp X

On November 11, wreathes are laid
     where spies once lived and learned their trade.
Camp X was once a prime location
     for those who worked to save our nation.

Y is for Yukon

To paddle the Yukon by canoe
would take at least two months to do.
But prospectors crossed it countless times
to find their fortunes in the mines.

Z is for Zero

Zero isn't zero; it tells you quite a lot.
Below is fairly chilly, above is really not.
Zero isn't zero; it's more vital than you think.
You need less than zero degrees to have yourself a rink.

A is for Aurora Borealis

Scientists say the Northern Lights are the result of particles from the atmospheres of the sun and the earth combining. The combination produces a spectacular light show with green, red, blue, and purple elements in the sky.

B is for Beaver

The hardworking beaver has been a favourite symbol even longer than Canada has been a nation. The first beaver postage stamp, the three-penny beaver, dates back to 1851. The beaver is also a good choice for a symbol because beavers are found in every province and territory in Canada.

C is for Canada

Canada, the second-largest country in landmass on earth, celebrates her 150th anniversary on July 1, 2017. The name Canada comes from the Iroquois word *kanata*. Native people have lived in Canada for more than 10,000 years.

D is for Dinosaur

If you are a dinosaur-lover the Badlands in Alberta is your destination. The town of Drumheller is the dinosaur capital of the world and boasts the world's biggest dinosaur skeleton. The Royal Tyrrell Museum, just west of Drumheller, has 40 dinosaur skeletons on display.

E is for Edgewalk

Edgewalk is a daring adventure for visitors to Toronto's CN Tower. Connected by safety wire and harness, visitors lean out over the city, 116 stories up. It is the tallest structure on earth where you are allowed to hang hands-free in the open air.

F is for Football

The Canadian Football League includes the BC Lions, Edmonton Eskimos, Calgary Stampeders, Saskatchewan Roughriders, Winnipeg Blue Bombers, Toronto Argonauts, Hamilton Tiger-Cats, Ottawa Redblacks, and Montreal Alouettes. The Grey Cup is a trophy that has been awarded to the top football team in Canada every year since 1909. It is called the Grey Cup because it was donated by Albert Grey, then Canada's Governor General.

G is for Gravy

For many, gravy is the best part of poutine. Poutine is made of french fries—or chips, as they are often called in Canada—cheese curds (chewy bits of cheese), and gravy. Many Canadians like to spice up their poutine with everything from bacon to onions and hot peppers.

H is for Husky

The name husky belongs to several dog breeds that were once very important for transportation and companionship in the North. Snowmobiles have replaced dog teams but huskies still race in competition and for fun. Huskies can be found all over North America and can manage warm weather because the same undercoat that keeps them warm in the winter keeps them cool in summer.

I is for Island Hymn

Lucy Maud Montgomery's song about her beloved PEI, Prince Edward Island, was adopted as the provincial song in 2010, 102 years after she wrote it. She came to be known worldwide for her beloved chapter book series, Anne of Green Gables.

J is for Blue Jays

The Toronto Blue Jays are Canada's only Major League baseball team. The Jays won the World Series in 1992 and 1993 and remain the only team from outside the United States to capture baseball's greatest prize. Their home field, the Rogers Centre, is on a street called Blue Jays Way.

K is for Klondike Days

Edmonton's K-Days festival is a 10-day exhibition and celebration of the city's role in the Klondike Gold Rush. The festival includes music, food booths, and yes, rides. The fair that became K-Days has been held at the Northlands site every year since 1910.

L is for Loonies and Toonies

The Royal Canadian Mint introduced the loonie to replace the fragile paper one-dollar bill in 1987. Its nickname came from the picture of a loon on one side. The toonie, a two-dollar piece, came into circulation in 1996.

M is for Maple Leaf

Canada has long been the destination for people who left their home countries in search of a better life. The leaf of the maple tree has symbolized Canada for more than 200 years. The image was put on the flag in 1965. One of the best parts of maple trees is the sap they make, which can be converted into delicious maple syrup.

N is for National Hockey League

An NHL team has lots of members behind the scenes. Aside from hockey players, there are people who sell tickets, drive the Zamboni to resurface the ice, and give play-by-play on television and radio. There are NHL hockey teams in Vancouver, Edmonton, Calgary, Winnipeg, Ottawa, Toronto, and Montreal.

O is for Osprey

The osprey, found in every continent except Antarctica, is the official bird of Nova Scotia. The osprey is an expert hunter that dives talons-first into water to pluck out fish. When an osprey chooses a mate, the pair stays together for life.

P is for Peary Caribou

Peary caribou can run as quickly as 80 kilometres per hour. They live in the Queen Elizabeth Islands, the farthest reaches of the Canadian north. With hooves shaped like shovels, the caribou scrape through snow to find herbs and grasses to eat.

Q is for Quebec City

Located on the banks of the St. Lawrence River, Quebec City is one of the most wonderful places in all of Canada. Founded more than 400 years ago, it stands as the capital of Quebec. The beautiful Château Frontenac is said to be the most-photographed hotel in the world.

R is for Rock Rabbits

The rock rabbit looks a bit like a chipmunk. It likes to hide near rocks so it favours Canada's many mountain ranges. When in danger, the rock rabbit emits a high-pitched squeak to warn its friends to take cover.

S is for Science Centre

Located in Toronto, the Ontario Science Centre gives visitors countless opportunities to see and touch exhibits that help explain how nature and technology work. The Centre, opened in 1969, is actually three separate buildings connected by bridges and escalators.

T is for Trout

Fishers and anglers love fishing for trout. Dolly Varden, brook, bull, and rainbow trout are prized catches but are often released back into the water to keep fish populations high. Eagles and bears enjoy eating trout as well.

U is for Underwear

Canada's most recognized underwear company is Stanfield's of Truro, Nova Scotia. Since 1906, the Stanfield's name has graced Canadian underwear. Company founder Charles Stanfield invented the "Drop Seat" one-piecer still in use today.

V is for Victoria

Victoria, the capital of British Columbia, has long been considered one of Canada's most beautiful cities. Nicknamed "The Garden City," Victoria is famous for its high tea served at the Empress Hotel and the Butchart Gardens, which includes a Children's Pavilion and a carousel. Nearly one million people visit the Gardens every year.

W is for Whale Watching

Whale watchers can see the huge mammal from several different vantage points: Nanaimo, BC, in the west to Churchill, Manitoba, in Central Canada, and the Cape Breton Highlands in Nova Scotia. While groups of fish are called schools, groups of whales are known as pods.

X is for Camp X

Spies from Britain, Canada, and the United States were trained in espionage during the Second World War at Camp X near Whitby, Ontario. The spies played an important part in the war effort. Every year a small group of supporters lays a wreath at the site where the compound once stood.

Y is for Yukon

The Yukon River is one of the greatest waterways in the world. The river begins in British Columbia and winds its way north to the Bering Sea in Alaska. It is more than 3,000 kilometres long and was used to transport miners and supplies during the Klondike Gold Rush (1896–1899).

Z is for Zero

Since 1970, Canada has used the metric system to gauge temperature, distance, and weight. Before that, Canadians used the Imperial system of pounds, miles, ounces, inches, and feet. In the metric system, water freezes at zero, and boils at 100 degrees Celsius.

*To Charlie, Ryan, Lily, and Zack, as well as Chuck and Dan,
whose love these children will forever carry in the marrow of
their bones. To Isla, about whom it can be said that only the
S is silent; Nikita, Teagan, Deo, Willow, Shea, and Stella.*

Mike

✳

*To my Deniau ancestor, who came from
France to Montreal, Quebec, in 1653.*

Sylvie

Sleeping Bear Press®

2395 South Huron Parkway, Suite 200
Ann Arbor, MI 48104
www.sleepingbearpress.com

Printed and bound in the United States.

10 9 8 7 6 5 4 3 2 1

Library of Congress Cataloging-in-Publication Data

Names: Ulmer, Michael, 1959- author. | Daigneault, Sylvie, illustrator.
Title: C is for Canada : celebrating our nation / written by Michael Ulmer ;
illustrated by Sylvie Daigneault.
Description: Ann Arbor, MI : Sleeping Bear Press, [2016] | Audience: Ages 6-10.
Identifiers: LCCN 2016026741 | ISBN 9781585369737
Subjects: LCSH: Canada—Juvenile literature. | Alphabet books.
Classification: LCC F1008.2 .U38 2016 | DDC 971—dc23
LC record available at https://lccn.loc.gov/2016026741